SPOTLIT GIRL

Wick Poetry Chapbook Series Four
Maggie Anderson, Editor

How to Paint the Savior Dead
Jason Gray

The Space Between Stars
Matt McBride

Spotlit Girl
Kevin Oberlin

SPOTLIT GIRL

Poems by Kevin Oberlin

The Kent State University Press
Kent, Ohio

Ohio Arts Council
A STATE AGENCY
THAT SUPPORTS PUBLIC
PROGRAMS IN THE ARTS

Library of Congress Catalog Card Number 2007044979
ISBN 978-0-87338-956-3
Manufactured in the United States of America

The Wick Poetry Series is sponsored in part by the
Wick Poetry Center at Kent State University.

Library of Congress Cataloging-in-Publication Data
Oberlin, Kevin.
    Spotlit girl : poems / by Kevin Oberlin.
            p. cm. — (Wick poetry chapbook series four ; 3)
    ISBN 978-0-87338-956-3 (pbk. : alk. paper) ∞
    I. Title.
PS3615.B474S65 2008
811'.6—dc22   2007044979
British Library Cataloging-in-Publication data are available.

12 11 10 09 08   5 4 3 2 1

CONTENTS

STAR-SPANGLED BANNER

"At Talladega you want to wear the red
lipstick, sweetie, red as Satan's tits,"
a well-tanned woman tells her. Already sweat
has soaked the pink bandana around her chest.
Oh God, she asks herself, *how did I
get here? My agent is so getting a phone call.*
Beers bounce from hand to hand and the sky
grumbles with jets. Soon the snarl of cars.
For holy Christ's sake, she sings jazz!
She's not some country floozie, liquored up
and bedding cowboys in her RV. She's got pizzazz.
And soul. No butter-blonde, this girl. She pulls
her red hair down and whips out sparks of red in the sun.
She was born in Texas, and Texas is where she's from.

COAST

"Just for shits and giggles, darlin', let's walk
to the end of the pier and back." Her mother swings
her beaded purse over her shoulder and talks
about the good of the salty air for singing.
"It also does wonders for the complexion, dear,
except the sun brings out your damn freckles,"
an automatic hand to the cleavage to clear
the crumbs of pigment covering her neck like pimples
of water or sand left by the spray of waves,
minute deposits of minerals. How will they look
in a dozen years? In twenty? Embedded in shale
as red as dirt, or as black as a coat of soot?
The seagulls circle above her, return to the ocean,
as the prairie grass shores the beach against her erosion.

SMILE

Monthly trips to the Smile Enhancement Studio
make her teeth a limerick, slick as leaves
exchanging news from further up the tree,
how at the top they've turned to expose their versos.
Yes, this is what she looks like at the bone,
a nervy girl, coy, compulsively neat,
plying her gums with cotton when she bleeds.
These cavities are sealed, oh subtle shrimp, oh know.
And still she prefers to smile without the teeth,
clean as they are. Her lips allure and kink
at their ends, unfold, unsquirm, and vilely curl,
or violently submit to being seen
like children raw with wants. Their faces skin
her secrets, how she craves to kill the world.

HOTEL

A lobby full of businesswomen in suits,
each of them an agent or go-between,
talking on cell phones, just being loud—
a girl could get lost in this crowd, recruited,
pushed through a rack of coats and never seen
except by other hostages lost for good.
She passes quickly by their skirted legs,
a ripple of silk from which she pulls her own
wireless and dials. After the distant ringing,
"Mom, you said you'd meet me here. I'm begging.
There's like a business convention going on,
and I can't find where I'm supposed to sing."
A briefcase catches her elbow, and the phone flips closed.
It's razor thin and goes wherever she goes.

CAB

"Mom, can you stay on the phone? There's this guy
across the street. I think he's watching me."
She can't tell if it's in her head or if his eyes
are following her, two black bubbles freed
from the hundreds glued to the stage that night.
In a crowd they seemed harmless, like fireflies
caught in the jar of her throat. But out in the streetlight
they're sinister. Maybe a fan, but maybe some sly
crazy who doesn't know she's someone who matters,
someone people would miss. She turns the corner
and listens for steps behind her, spots a cab
at the curb ahead. "Hey Mom, I think he's gone,
and I've got a cab. I'll see you at the hotel?"
The cabbie's heard of her and gets tipped well.

WORKOUT

In the weight room everyone has a bottle
of water close by, an iPod, and often a trainer
keeping the count with such enthusiasm the spotter,
who looks like his arms are full of birds swaddled
in muscle shirts, can hardly keep from laughing.
Her Hollywood beau is clumsy under the bars,
a stringy boy, a scrapper bulking up, mashing
his palms against the metal. He's got a part
as an action hero's son. She usually keeps
to spinning class, but today she's decided to stay
to imagine herself atop him, inserted between
the bar and his body. She thinks of the love they'd make,
the feathery tease of her gym shorts over his leanness,
the work of his thighs between her angled knees.

LICENSE

She's old enough now to drive herself
to rehearsals with B. B. King and Billy Joel
when Warner Bros. doesn't send the limo.
It sometimes makes her feel like someone else,
the warmth of imported skins kissing her neck
and some designer's dress that makes her whole
body feel its slinkiness past control.
Inside, her bones jangle against themselves.

Much better to wear the jeans she's broken in,
and better to have her own hands on the wheel.
No one's listening here as she warms up
to the radio, belting between the staves of wind
whatever harmonies she chooses to throw her secret
throat open, until she commands them to stop.

POKER FACE

A half smile like when she's singing sometimes,
a couple of fingers slipped in the folds of her dress.
She sometimes closes her eyes a good long while.
Around the table, nobody thinks her wise
enough to fold a pair in the blind, the loss
too much to bear. She loves to collect her stash,
the tickle of felt on her arm in motion across
the smooth table. Sometimes she has to laugh
out loud in the middle of someone else's joke,
the careless trickle of chips. Her daddy taught her
not to play with her hair or twist it like rope.
"You think you're cute, but those are your tells, right there."
She pulls her hair and winks, then smiles sadly.
These men around the table ain't her daddy.

SOLO FOR LOVERS

She'd like to sing in front of a red curtain,
in its curves the undisclosed crack of the snare
to accent her finger snaps, her outstretched arm,
a little wrist to say you're here to see
her upstage cross and curtsy, not the men
in white suits who flash their brassy bells
with the beat, who bob and sway beneath her,
the little razz that licks up into a swell.
Make no mistake, the world drifts, afloat
on her, the gents with their polite erections,
all those trumpets and drums, their wives flushed
and unspooling while she salts the good places.
You have to take the opportunity, young lovers,
to be that sequined, spotlit girl, to be her.

MISTAKES

Paws up, she's jimmied free of the blouse,
has got her dress robes on in fine flight
past the union guys winding cable, and right
into the arms of her mother, eyes soaked.
Her mother knows not to ask the trouble.
It must have been a terrible performance,
a miscue, or a sustained note broken by chance
intervention of memory, a bruised arm bubbling
up from her melodies' soporific drive.
"I made so many goddamn mistakes up there,"
her sobbing gutters to breath, a smooth purr.
Her mother bandages her with a hug and sighs
into hair curled and hardened with sprays and mousse,
"The only one who notices is you."

WISDOM

Through the blood of ether, a gag of copper gauze
collects in her throat. "Oh God, these cheeks, they'll say
they're 'ruddy,' or worse, 'sanguine,'" words she can't
remember picking up, but now in the haze
they're clear as the nurse's assurance nothing connects
her wisdom teeth to her voice, a latex glove
stroking her arm. But surely she must be infected,
face scarred from all the hands in her mouth,
the claw of scrapeful tools, the gulp of cutting.
She knows it's there, even though she's under,
like when she opens her eyes and finds she's kissing,
hungrily close, the scored lips of the trumpeter.
It's just a metaphor for making music, she knows,
and yet her voice, so small she must have swallowed.

FLORIDA

Her daddy loves these Jimmy Buffet dives
with their double-fried fish, coconut-crusted
snapper and shellfish, the way the menu describes
its drinks like steel drums, but they come rusty.
There is no Florida in her blood, no puerile whisper
in the violet, nothing east of New Orleans pomp.
Texas trails off into the plains, the white
sands along her shoulders, ends in swamp.
"You and me, there's hurricanes between us,
sometimes, and I'm sorry," he sips his margarita.
She knows when he says this not to discuss
the burly swell of oranges in California.
She loves him still. Though she's acquired taste,
he's the golden drawl that silhouettes her face.

OPENER

"Opening for B. B. King is like getting felt up
by Pavarotti: sort of a brush with the elect,
but not that good for your self-esteem, a flop
in a little city." Her anger's only in check
because the bad connection makes her focus
to hear what the promoter says at all.
Grounded for half an hour to wait for big gusts
of wind or some shit, she figures she'll can
this project well before the plane takes off.
She drops the phone a moment, lets the guy
talk to the tray while she collects a coke
from an attendant with sympathetic eyebrows.
The promoter's jokes are too true to be funny,
and she thinks he's fresher with her than he ought to be.

ICE CREAM

Because she comes out singing, the ice cream man
loves her and sells her chocolate-covered cones
half price for any neighborhood kids that scam
along next to her. Here she's been on radio,
so all their mothers think she's good and rich.
What do these women tell their pudgy-eyed dolls
with Texan drawls stuffed in their mouths like whipped
cream in a donut? "Keep close to that girl, y'all,
go tug on her dress and see if she'll get you a treat.
Maybe someday she'll bring you into the fold."
She doesn't bother to count their heads, just keeps
buying until their hands are full. The bolder
girls are placing orders, but the little boys stare,
openmouthed, at her body, her smile, her hair.

SWEET TEA

Strange to sit on the porch in the afternoon
watching the drizzles of condensation relax
and fall when she knows the post won't come
with anything for her. Maybe she'll get a fax
from her agent if something important comes in the bags
of daily fan mail the interns filter through.
Her agent always says there are bags, but maybe
there's only letters from kids, or a few blue
poems from perverts. She tears a leaf of mint
and stirs it into her glass to diffuse its flavor.
The phone's been quiet all day, so no new gigs.
This isn't how the A-list works, she's sure,
watching the neighbors' cars tool the suburbs
and any moment her mother home for supper.

WATER

Around eleven o'clock she stops loving
the way the cattail down catches in the grass,
thick as hair around the edge of the pond.
She'll have to call her agent, take a pass
on songs by composers still alive, their slacks
and shirts rumpled with lack of sleep and not
from making love. She'd better stick with classics,
the margins of scores smudged with oily spots
from fingers well-traveled along their narrow roads.
They know familiarity wears better than fame
when pressed into the cleft of a grand piano,
the lights trailing off to some corner of the stage.
No suckers for reeds in the waters she used to wade,
thinking when they dried up she'd remain.

STORM

The thunder hulks, then rushes up beneath
the steady bass line, locking its own groove
into the stage's foundations. She bares her teeth
in an uninhibited smile, unshaken, though moved.
No disrespect meant to all the fine concert halls
across the United States, Europe, and Australia,
their carefully crafted ceilings reflecting all
her melody's perfect hips and sighs, the regalia
of quick breaths caught up in the moments she makes.
But she likes it better, singing with the weather outside
where the small audience gets up when the ground shakes
and pushes forward under the lip of the shell to hide,
so close she sees their faces, and they feel her warmth.
Any moment now it's going to pour.

CRY

"Baby," she sings as if her mouth were full
of bubbles, smooth and round, reflecting light
gently as planets do. It's late at night.
The cymbals rattle and rise, the final push
into the note she pulls from somewhere below
her chest, like a bottle before the stopper's out.
Maybe during the applause a man in the crowd
will whisper, "Baby." Sometimes someone shouts
before she's even in full voice, a cry
that makes her body quiver. A lover makes
a sound like that. So many lovers, the heart
mistakes her music for its own. "Don't you cry,"
she sings, and in the "I" for a moment her voice breaks,
the space between notes where her body pulls apart.